there's only one way this is going to end

john sweet

ISBN: 978-81-19228-13-3

First Edition: 2023
Rs. 200/-

Cyberwit.net
HIG 45 Kaushambi Kunj, Kalindipuram
Allahabad - 211011 (U.P.) India
http://www.cyberwit.net
Tel: +(91) 9415091004
E-mail: info@cyberwit.net

Printed at VCORE.

Many thanks to the

following publications, where

some of these poems first

appeared:

BlazeVox

Dreich Mag

Ginosko

Otoliths

Phenomenal Literature

Quail Belle

Contents

i. static poured out of the hole in his heart

eating the bones of the poem

suicide factory,
6 a.m.,
and rothko is always waiting at the door

has his pills and his
ideas about transcendence

wants to paint you
in shades of black and grey

wants me to listen to the sound of
razor blades through bare flesh

calls it music and he calls it holy and
what matters here is that i am
less than i was
when you and i were together

what matters here is the possibility
that the pale blurred sunlight
of my childhood might return

that the dead lawns up and
down this bitter street are
nothing more than premonitions

after fifteen years of february
i am ready to start breathing again

holy, holy

and we are believers in beauty
                    you and i
and in the necessity of violence

we are more than christ and
we are better than god but
this is nothing special

all hearts are failures

all sunlight matters

you start with faith and you
end at war and
no one who wants your vote
is ever your friend

no one who brings you the
news of your father's death
will stay for the feast

and all of it hurts
                yes
but only some of it is
meant to be personal

lin

in love with you on
charlotte street, in the
shadows of ruined empires, and
still young enough to think
that this matters

kissing you naked in the
blind heat of august afternoons
and then tasting your sweat

drinking it like the
one true religion

air around us thick with
sunlight & dust and the
scent of spanish flowers

anodyne

suicide factory 6 a.m. and all of
my ex-lovers are there with
whatever pawns they married

all of my sorrow is left crippled and
broken beneath harsh
fluorescent lights, and is any of this the truth?

has it ever really been necessary
for the years to
pass in chronological order?

and no matter what you answer,
i wake up lost almost every morning

litany of concentric circles

finished his drink then
shot himself

said he hoped the poem would be better than the
shit i usually wrote but i didn't even
know him, wasn't even there, and he pulled the
trigger and it was november

was sunlit and cold and the blood on the
walls, sound of the girl smiling in the doorway
of the porn shop and my car wasn't running again

was rusting in the sunlight of someone else's
driveway and the sound of the
shot and she was smiling as i walked by, was sharing a
cigarette with the guy who worked there, asked me
how the poem was going, said she wasn't even there but
he had finished the drink then shot himself and
past the high school was the river

sunlit and cold and i found his body floating
near the shore, knew his girlfriend but i couldn't
lift him up and two kids on the bridge above
throwing rocks down at us, tried to explain that i
wasn't there, that i wasn't here, but my
hands had lost all feeling

mouth was bleeding and the hole in the side of his
head where the light poured out, said the girl
had been his sister and i told him he was dead

do you remember?

it was november, bright blue sky and frozen and
he'd written his girlfriend a letter, had told her
he was sorry and then he pulled the trigger

told her to ask me about the poem

showed her some words i'd scribbled across the backs of
some carry-out menus when i found her
standing in the doorway of the mexican restaurant,
explained that i wasn't even there, and these kids
across the street throwing rocks at us

my car down by the river, *tangled up in blue*
on the radio and she said she'd always hated dylan,
said she'd always hated the stones, and then he
finished his drink and pulled the trigger

static poured out of the hole in his heart and
he said the poem was the important thing

said the gun was just a metaphor but
he wouldn't stop bleeding

laughed when i showed him what i'd written
and told me i'd better try again

summer '94

says *john i might be*
dying but at least i'm not a
coward and we're back on
charlotte street here

we're drunk at two in the afternoon
and i say *maybe*

i say *maybe* and then i pause and
then i say *maybe*

i say *maybe, but the survivors*
are the ones who get to
write history and he laughs

      he laughs

says *point for you* and
i say *maybe*

i say nothing

sit there with a warm beer in my
hand and wait for a
better way to waste my life

the future written in your blood, not mine

a child drowned in
the father's heart

a fist and then an apology
and then a fist again

war on a more
intimate level

patriotism
in place of art

when the enemy is on
                all sides
there is nothing left
but to shoot in
every direction

a cubist sonnet for the last days of empire

dog is shot at the
far end of the street
in the last days of summer

blue sky or silver and
chromium sun and the dog is
shot and the sound of laughter

the body of the dog and
of the old man

the mother pushing the
baby but not the baby

not the dog

and the trigger is pulled and
the silence is
what you'd expect

faint hum of traffic

dog barking in the distance
but the
trigger has been pulled

the dog has been shot

body of the mother lying at
an awkward angle at
the far end of the street

the baby crying

the old man

and it feels as if something
terrible
is about to happen

fragment, early autumn or late winter

this quiet sense of
                joy, then

something new
and i give thanks

relearn the subtle shape
of hope and hold it up
to the dying sun

[out of our minds and out of our league]

feels good or at least not
like dying and
that's gotta count for something

end of the line of a family of
junkies and alkies and suicides, and
he remembers a teacher, 2nd or
3rd grade

smiles and the scent of lilacs and
she always told him that
everyone got to choose their own future

and maybe she even believed it

and forty years later he
keeps having the same dream, the
severed hands and the burning house

keeps waking up in a strange room
next to someone else's wife

and there is never any sound but
the sound of time running out

st marie and her holy light

the emperor of
the city of dust on a
bitter sunlit afternoon in
                    january

empty streets past
bankrupt buildings or
the shadows of ghosts
as they starve

saw a movie like this once and
remembered the ending
from my childhood

four below zero and a
faceless stranger knocking on
the door of an empty house

steady hum of silence
caught in my throat

i have always been
afraid of the smothering
weight of the
future

a vast conspiracy

or you with your ideas about
love, or me
with my fear of open spaces

three weeks of rain and snow and
the subtle way i keep moving closer to
an admission of defeat

look

the brakes are shot and
the washing machine leaks

the concept of forward motion is
something to consider, but
inertia has its own attractions too

woman wakes up on easter sunday,
sets her child on fire,
and what are your options?

what are we really talking about
when we discuss our dreams?

or maybe one of us just wants
the other to crawl over broken glass
to make some obscure point

maybe the drugs we've
always sworn by
no longer make us happy

maybe they never did

and we thought that when the war was over the blood would all flow backwards, and we were wrong

or living like a wounded animal, which
isn't really the same thing as living,
but there you are in your collapsing hole
with your open wounds and your blood trail

here we are after 25 years of winter

½ a lifetime spent digging at the same
small patch of frozen ground with bare hands

low tide

faulty compass

and what i find out too late is
that anger isn't enough

is that silence isn't an alternative to
suicide, but a slower version of it and so
                              we scream

we make ourselves such easy targets

open the door and all of that pale, blinding
sunlight just blows holes straight through you

save us all from love and hope

was breathing in the tarnished weight of silver skies,
was trapped there between forgetting and forgotten,
21 years of pointless starvation,
air thick with the approach of rain,
distant pulse of passing trains,
and the child in the back seat made no sound

had no hands

looked a little like me, but i no longer took
responsibility for any of the pain in the world

i no longer walked
when it was easier to crawl

had finally become my father

terminal song for cautious martyrs

dirty snow and dead lawns in these
final days of someone's life and
does it matter whose?

not really

know that you're loved and
know that you're doomed

move in the spaces
between houses

between cities

and tell me your secrets
but not that you love me

not that you need me

we are too far out to sea for
so much useless weight

knives, deeper

in the act of failure,
salvation

in the hands, in the heart, in this
mouth filled with sharpened teeth

words,
but not my own

a warmer violence

sunlight or a bleeding fist

a thought,
but turned outward,
twisted, stretched into
some new shape

the highway maybe, where it
arcs out around the city

the city as it falls into ruin

a cancer? a virus?

slow decay, in any event, with the
houses all collapsing in on
themselves, the cellars filled
with bones, old yearbooks, baby shoes

the past is the enemy, of course,
because everyone dies

love?

a theory, maybe,
but not a solution,
and then what?

fortune

or else you wake up easter morning in
some stranger's bed and try to
remember her name

try to remember what comes between
the past and the future or
how to explain tanguy's theories on these distances

his unexpected death and then cobain's suicide
and all the reasons your father has
given up on you

all of the roads you could take to
get back to your wife,
        your children
         your house full of tiny fires,
  or maybe it's just time to walk away

to maybe just pull your lover closer
                and breathe

and no matter what happens,
this moment has already become
the beginning of some slow
and crippling end

i am the sky, we were the rain

the trick is fear
mixed with sorrow

the trick is despair held up
to the warm spring sun

your lover, naked,
wrapped in cords of light

and i sat there in the
falling house and thought about
writing a poem, but
i couldn't even breathe

i had no idea where the money
for the mortgage would come from

had no idea why peace could
could only be achieved
through war

couldn't begin to think of
how i'd explain my
failures to my children

a love poem from the upstate desert, late february

and now nothing means anything

north of the city, late february, wastelands and
industrial parks and nothing quite living
and nothing quite dead

each sunfilled day an
infinite weight on the chest

each passing moment, and
what to do but drive?

shades of luminous grey layered over
shades of luminous grey, and that
the rain here tastes like poison

that you learn to accept it

and this is the plan, okay?

this is the nothing from nothing that
will come to define all of our lives

not freedom but the
freedom to consume

the need for more even in this
manmade wasteland, and have i failed my

children or was it my own children
who failed me?

i'm told the distinction matters

i'm told that all wars can be won,
but who are you willing to sacrifice?

who do you love more
than yourself?

everyone lies at
some point

nov17

grey rain on the
village of severed hands

victim found face down in a
ditch in the last light of all-saints day and
your father further up north or
maybe way out west

sends postcards of
sunlight and marigolds

sends rumors of his own
unexpected death but
when you call
your mother never answers the phone

the war drags on long after
the last village has been
burned to the ground

the days are never as hopeless as
you remember them but
we're still a long way from home

a tyrant on fire, let his burning heart warm our bones

your life, amounting to less than
the sum of passing days

faith in a savior who
couldn't even save himself,
and is this a joke?

a religion based on torture

a nation dedicated to
the idea of witch hunts

if fear is what you value most
then i was born to be your enemy

the other truth

honey loves her burning house says
she loves her father's fists, says
the dream doesn't mean anything

tell her the baby's dead, tell her
her boyfriend's a thief,
but all she wants to do is sing

all she wants to do is sleep

wake up smiling,
wipe the ashes from her eyes

the known

and then afternoon sunlight too
late to offer any warmth and then the
shadows of minor ghosts and
falling houses

the idea of hope
which gets harder to embrace

empty chairs in empty back yards

false visions

the death of the oldest child
which hasn't happened yet but
the image is unshakable

body curled up tightly in
some dark and filthy corner

the smell of ammonia

sound of a car door closing and
then a stranger's face
at the window

says he's brought us all luck but
his hands are
bloodstained and empty

ii. in the spaces between houses

a steady, slow descent

into the season of
dead lawns, then

of missing husbands and
runaway teenage daughters, and i am
not prophesying my own death here, i am
not expecting its sudden unannounced arrival,
but the idea still exists

weeds choke the flowers

a house at the other end of this
nowhere street burns to the ground

phosphorescent sun in a silver sky,
and that i am tired of talking about escape,
but it beats having to listen to
someone else's lies

i am tired of breathing, but it
seems like a lot of goddamn work
to make myself stop

seems like a temporary pause is
better than an absolute ending

show me how to accomplish
both at once,
and i will make you my god

self-portrait with tar

and words aren't actions,
and prayer is as
meaningless as regret

the temperature is nervous
stutter between rain and snow

the town is a vast expanse of
empty parking lots, of
grey shot through with crushed
plastic and dead leaves

i have wasted my life

i am afraid of growing old and
dying in front of my children

i am afraid of
growing old and dying

in the end we are only
something
subtracted from nothing

imagined landscape no. 1

and there is nothing you
can love in this world that
you can't be taught to hate and
there is nothing so beautiful
that it can't be made ugly

there are obvious reasons
why we fear losing
everything we think we have

this last part is what i
remember you telling me
just before you left

st. elizabeth, crowned w/ tears of joy

eyes filled w/
sunlight & flowers &
      never grow old

never burn down

only dream w/ yr
heart in my hands

torch

in that moment before the last one, right
there, three a.m. with the machines
all turned off and the hallways echoing with the
footsteps of dying women, women with the
heads of dogs, of birds, of minotaurs, and i
turned to you and asked *is he dead?* and i turned
to you and asked *are we there yet?* and
you smiled, you were crying, were pulling tiny
crosses from your hair, the bones of minor
gods, had the gun aimed towards the sky,
warm sunlight like the sticky hands of priests
down the lengths of our naked bodies, and
we were fucking when the woman was
discovered missing, you were bent over and
hanging onto the refrigerator and the baby
was crying, was saying something about
mommy, about the stains on the rug, nothing
that made any sense and the room stank of
bleach, and when you came it was like
the war was finally over

when the moment arrived, none of us
thought it would matter

we just stood there talking while
the north tower fell

heretic

collision isn't fatal but
the blood offers possibilities

tv on the wrong channel and
the president speaks of raping babies

shouts about the importance of wealth,
the need for vengeance,
the illusion of victory and
everything spoken through a
mouthful of sawdust and dogshit and
then the man with the gun laughs

says there's no such thing
as something new

says this, and then he takes
his own life and, in a world without
safety, there can only be promises
kept or promises broken

can only be darker shades of
grey and red

the two of us alone in a
stranger's room and
waiting for the first light of day

with broken wings, with bruised hearts

& the future is prisons, you see,
and the future is loss

let go of yr house, of yr
children, but hang onto the hatred
                    that defines you

give up christ

give up all those pretty songs
your mother used to sing

close in on holiness
like a soldier taking aim

mondrian, through the big window

glare of white sky on chrome
                on broken glass
                on hills made of gauze

streets and then
roads and then highways

cities and the vast
empty spaces between them

dogs chained to dying trees

stand far enough away from
the pain and the desolation and
look for a pattern

look for the source
of the bleeding

imagine the truth but
remember that i know your
lies as well as i know my own

imagine beauty

steal what you can before
grief is all we
have left

a quiet man's suicide in the age of disconnect

and then saturday, sunlit and cold,
and then sunday

the plague of christ and
the relentless weight of junkies

taste of your salt on my fingers

lust or love, and
does it matter which?

aren't they the same in the end?

start with pure blue sky then
add the truth
and you're halfway there

songs by dead heretics for secret lovers

hearts and bones and
sleeping children and i remember i was high,
was still waiting for your birth

i remember promising to never
cause you any pain but
this was later, after the meanings of words
had become blurred

all of those drunken narcissists
who swore they were poets

all those unmarked graves dug up
on the western edge of town

there is no point to history if
all we do is live through it

do you see?

forward and backward are meaningless
once the maps have been burned

the war is won and lost
simultaneously
and then it's forgotten

weapons are improved

lists of the missing are updated

do you care?

it's polite to say you do but
fuck the niceties

the dogs understand survival

no one needs to starve in a
world filled with corpses

no one dies of thirst
in an ocean of blood

do you see the possibilities?

not joy, but joy
derived from strength,
from the suffering of others

not peace,
but fear in all forms

the slavery of spirit
and then of body

the map, yes,
and then the map within

all directions leading toward *lost*

all clocks run out

zero becomes the answer,
no matter the question

all of us seen through the distorted lens of fear

frost on your lover's fingertips on
sunday morning and
kisses that taste like depression

pure white light and a ring around the sun
that breaks your heart

did you bring gifts?

was the war delayed until the baby was
well enough to be killed?

or maybe the house is filled with
beautiful objects that have no use

maybe the poem is written in
rust-colored blood
on a pale blue bedroom wall

the important thing is that
someone here feels pain

gift

or beauty arriving almost
                    too late, or
                            hope

the idea of being in love because
all other choices are meaningless

the fear of missing out
on sunlit warmth

no casual joy, no
meaningful deaths, right?

all scars kissed

all motion stopped

let me hold you in this silent room,
on this cautious afternoon

let me breathe into the
thought of you breathing into me

let the two of us be
all we ever need

the captain, the sinking ship

and we will do something or
            better yet
we will do nothing
and the lawns will all be green

the doors will be kicked in
and the children dragged
out into the streets

the votes recounted

zero for you and zero for
them and then none for me

let all sounds be the sound of freedom

these houses and
the spaces between them

these streets all heavy with silence
in the early afternoon

trees and the shadows of trees
and the ghost of de chirico

a kingdom of dust
for the lucky few

can't be god these days unless you're
willing to bleed and
maybe that's how it always was

not every cripple is a prophet

not every prophet understands
the necessity of hope

picture yourself as the desert
and your life
finally starts to make sense

[let all ideas be sacred]

there is no philosophy here,
no theology,
there are only the passing days

the fine art of survival,
which fails us all in the end, and what i
miss isn't my father but my
anger towards him

the idea of myself as
someone i no longer am

and who is it in this empty room that
finds humor in a failed suicide,
and who is it that finds hope?

which cup do you choose to drink from
when one is filled with blood
and the other with sand?

why do you worry about your death
when your life is
still waiting for meaning?

or when i was a child

not living but
hiding in shades of grey, in
rooms with cracked and peeling walls,
with water-stained ceilings and
not drowning but not
breathing either

not looking at the sky but
staring directly into the dying sun

falling slowly into the frozen river
from a great height

like all good pain,
it only lasts for a second

in the kingdom of the sleeping heart

or the strangeness of a pain that
lingers for ten years, for
twenty, that colors my memories and
stains the sky, or the idea of
hope placed against the idea of
hopelessness to create a house
that will never stand

no one tells you they love you because
they love you, but only to
have you give their gift back to them

there are worse crimes

there are silences too deep to
ever find the bottom of

you swim in them until you
drown
or else you fight your way to the surface

you look for
land in every direction

it's never as close as you'd hoped,
                              but it's there

poem, 20 years later

and you were
beautiful and i was blind and
time only ever moved in
            one direction

only ever pulled us
            further apart

footnote to the fine art of starvation

thought i was the river
through the desert of your heart

thought i was going to be or that
we were going to become

that the kingdom
wouldn't need walls

the two of us safe within our
hearts and laughing at the
idea of ever having to
do without

hymn

she says *let's pretend*
you're not my god
and he laughs

says *let's forget that the*
planes will crash or that
the baby will need a name and
she says these things and
the sky fills with rain

she believes in the future
even after it's
proven to be a lie

this is how he knows
he loves her

a gift for st marie

and if the house is not a
home and if the distance between
us keeps growing

if christ is an
unwanted child on fire

i hold him close like
a lover

i drink the poison he
offers and we both laugh

we both bleed but only
one of us bleeds for you

only one of us understands
the true nature of faith

the exile, upon arrival

the city is what i thought it would be,
and i live here
expecting to not be found

the sky is dull pewter,
streaked with dust,
and the sun is only itself

watery shadows in
the spaces between houses,
down these streets with their
dead-end futures bound to their empty pasts

no escape and no retreat

the steady heat of decay but
no warmth
and that i am not a god

am not a priest, but a
poet maybe?

no,
i am not a poet

am a failure, i guess,
but not at anything in particular

a man in hiding, but still
these people find me

long-lost drinking buddies and
deadbeats with hungry eyes

the underage sisters of ex-girlfriends
and they tell me they love me

they tell me they need to get high

need money for their babies
but i'm not listening

i'm late for work

the rent is due

always some minor crisis

the father, the son, the holy ghost and
one of them says he knows i've been
fucking his wife but i haven't

i'm in hiding here

i've learned the secret world of weedy
back yards and back alleys, of vacant lots and
the muttered silences beneath bridges

POINT A to *POINT B* and
am i father?

depends on who you ask

a coward, yes, and a prophet,
but the truths i foretell are still
20 years away at this point

the sound of the freeway is a muted thing,
the sound of distant surf,
of whispered conversations in a cemetery and
are we strangers, you and i?

i think maybe we've known each other
in some version of the past

think maybe we've both slammed too many
doors in anger to find our way back to
whatever rooms we have in common

loss is the great equalizer and
regret the perfect fuel for all of these
machines we've built to go nowhere in,
and cassie laughs when she reads this

says maybe i'm a philosopher

says maybe i'm a failed suicide,
which is probably more interesting,
but i am not a conquistador

i am not a politician,
not a whore or a martyr

i am less than whatever i've
been accused of being and i am more than
what i've been given credit for and
the city is what i need it to be

the sky here is always
a calming shade of poison and
each prayer a shadow in a
shadowless world

and i understand the need for victims,
but i refuse to be one

hope will be enough to get us through
until the exact moment that
it no longer is

do you believe me?

seems odd that we have these choices

an obvious answer and a wrong one
and we blow it every time

we speak too soon or we wait too long

the words get caught

i hate you or *i love you* or
some other meaningless drivel and
the city keeps changing by
staying the same

i define myself by the
failures of those who accuse me of
being a failure

we will all learn what it
means to be lost

3rd

in love then with the teenager you were and
possibly even the woman you'd become

afraid of the future or
maybe just unprepared

maybe just unaware that all of the
promised choices were lies,
that all options could be whittle down to
                            LIVE or DIE,
          but i remember your beauty

i remember the heat of the sun

it was enough to bring me
to this moment without regret

where we stand, or where we kneel

a lover's leap or a
murder/suicide or this man on the
32nd floor with enough firepower to
                              win a war

you kill those who would take your freedom
and then you kill those who say they have none

you kill the children because
children grow up filled with ideas of revenge,
and do you really needs reasons for
your actions when you hold all the power?

is there really such a thing as a
savior who might actually care?

all any of us can ever know for sure
is that everyone else is wrong